BETHLEHEM'S ROAD

A journey through Advent

RAY SIMPSON

kevin
mayhew

First published in Great Britain in 2017 by Kevin Mayhew Ltd
Buxhall, Stowmarket, Suffolk IP14 3BW
Tel: +44 (0) 1449 737978 Fax: +44 (0) 1449 737834
E-mail: info@kevinmayhew.com

www.kevinmayhew.com

9 8 7 6 5 4 3 2 1 0

ISBN 978 1 84867 909 2
Catalogue No. 1501548

Cover design by Rob Mortonson
© Image used under licence from Shutterstock Inc.
Edited by Virginia Rounding
Typeset by Angela Selfe

Printed and bound in Great Britain

Contents

DECADE THREE
Make ready for the Coming

DECADE FOUR
Glimpses of glory

About the author

Ray Simpson is a Celtic new monastic for tomorrow's world, a lecturer, consultant, liturgist, and author of some 30 books. He is the founding guardian of the international Community of Aidan and Hilda (a dispersed inter-church movement which is also an Acknowledged Anglican Community) and the pioneer of its e-studies programmes. He is an Anglican priest who was commissioned to work for Free and Roman Catholic churches in a unique experiment. Ray has authored over thirty books of contemporary worship, Celtic spirituality and prophetic challenge. He lectures and offers leaders' retreats in several continents and on the Holy Island of Lindisfarne. He writes a weekly blog on www.raysimpson.org

Prologue

The word Advent means Coming. What or who is coming? We may sense a wonder and a mystery, but if we are in the wrong place, or in an unreceptive frame of mind, or just too busy, we may miss it. So Advent must also be about our own preparation for the Coming.

In the first ten of our forty daily reflections, we will look out for road blocks that prevent the Coming. We will clear them away.

In the following ten days, we will search for signposts – prophecies, intuitions, stirrings – that help us travel in the direction of what or who is to come.

The Coming is a mystery, but a bit here and a bit there is revealed to those who are prepared. For ten days, we explore how we may make ready for the Coming One.

In the final ten days, we will discover glimpses of glory – fresh expressions of the Light of the World. Perhaps we can scent, sense, embrace them. We will learn to improve our seeing. We will allow these fresh expressions of the Light to transform us so that we become part of the story.

We suggest that you read the reflection, the Bible passage and the prayer once, and then read them again slowly, taking time to meditate and apply them, and to make the prayer your own response to God.

Readers may either start on 15 November and finish at Christmas, or start on 29 November and finish at Epiphany.

DECADE ONE

Roadblocks to the Coming

1. Grooves

When rebels wish to prevent a significant figure from coming to their town they erect road blocks. The rebel within each of us treats God like that. The 'road blocks' we can erect are many and devious. Sometimes they may be unacknowledged and individual. A road block may even take the form of living in a groove.

'We've always done things this way, vicar, and we always will.' If we are in a groove, we can't see what is outside it. We miss a world of possibility. To be stuck in a groove is to be trapped in an empty routine or a dead end. Life goes round and round in the same old circle. We are like Shakespeare's Macbeth who says 'I am cabined, cribbed, confined . . .' (Act 3 Scene 4).

Prophets like Isaiah and John the Baptist call us to clear a way for God to move among us (Isaiah 40:3 and Mark 1:3) but we can't make a way if we are stuck in a groove or if, like the ostrich, we keep our head in the sand. When we do that, Advent becomes a non-event.

In contrast to the groove mentality is lateral thinking. Vertical thinking is sticking with the current approach, being rigid. Lateral thinking is coming at a problem from a different direction with a flexible mindset. I once confided in a gym instructor that I was tired of the same stale fitness routines. 'Next time you come, imagine you are a child,' she suggested, 'bounce and jump on the trampoline in all directions and enjoy yourself.'

Most people did not see Jesus' birth in a smelly stable because they were too snooty to look for it in such a place. They were in a groove. They had tunnel vision.

Step back and look at life from a different perspective. Place a grain or a flower in your hand and slowly repeat:

To see a World in a Grain of Sand
And a Heaven in a Wild Flower,
Hold Infinity in the palm of your hand
And Eternity in an hour.[1]

John, the author of The Book of Revelation, suggests that eventually every eye will see Jesus. But what a tragedy if we leave it too late for this life, if we only see him, from a distance, as a defeated rebel. Ask God to give you the eyes of a child now.

Bible reading
Revelation 1:7, 8

Prayer
Open our eyes that we may see.
Touch our hearts that we may feel.
Move our legs that we may leap towards you.

---

1. From William Blake's *Auguries of Innocence.*

2. Greed

When our lives are all about possessing, things pile up. They obstruct the One who Comes. When our lives are all about getting, we miss the fact that real life is about giving. The deepest reality people seek, the One we all long for, even if we do not know it, comes to us as gift. A Christmas present of a Russian Matryoshka doll is a gift within a gift. God's world is like a ball that is a gift. The gift is hidden within a gift.

Alexander Schmemann, in his book *The Life of the World*, writes:

> All that exists is God's gift to man, and it all exists to make God known to man, to make man's life communion with God ... God blesses everything He creates, and, in biblical language, this means that He makes all creation the sign and means of His presence and wisdom, love and revelation.[2]

In Chapter 12 of his Gospel, Luke records some warnings of Jesus. Today's Bible passage is known as The Parable of the Rich Fool. It is a warning against putting trust in riches. It reflects a tendency we all have. Our thoughts and actions, perhaps unconsciously, are governed by 'I want more'. We want more to satisfy our appetites, but also out of fear. We acquire things as a hedge against loss. We deceive ourselves that we can hang on to things, or hibernate inside our store houses.

The truth is that food does not last. Houses and family arrangements do not last. Jobs and social structures do not last. We do not last. All die.

---

2. Alexander Schmemann, *The Life of the World*, St Vladimir's Seminary Press, Crestwood, New York, 2000.

If we live in the illusion that things last, when we die God will say to us: 'You fool! This very night your life is being demanded of you. And the things you have prepared, whose will they be?' (Luke 12:20).

How may we come to the place where we experience all as gift?

1. Place into a mental bin things you wish to possess and in which you put your trust.

2. Become aware of trees, birds, grass ... the air you breathe, and thank God for them.

3. Become aware of what is given to you – for example, life, calling, love ...

Bible reading
Read and reflect on Luke 12:13-21.

Prayer
Come, Justice Restorer, chastise producers who applaud free markets but create monopolies and overprice their products.

Come, Divine Gift, may I cease to vainly strive,
may I relax into what comes as gift,
may I be ready for the thankful embrace.

3. Grumbling

Grumbling, or miserableness, is not a condition we can't help – it is a choice we make. This famous anonymous saying illustrates this truth: 'Two prisoners behind bars, one saw mud, the others stars.'[3] We can miss the stars, and whatever they may tell us about what is coming, if we look down on people or are like bad work persons who blame their tools. If we are tight-lipped and tight-fisted, we dismiss Christ when he comes in the guise of the stranger at the door.

Grumbling is a choice. It tends to look for the worst side of any situation or person, in order to complain. If it is indulged in often, it can become a default position, a way of life. A sullen mood leads to a sullen face that creates a sullen atmosphere.

Joy cannot dance in such an atmosphere, nor can the King appear. We grumble about the neighbours, old people, young people, other people in general. We grumble about food, work, aches and pains, the government, the council – you name it.

Miserableness, variously known as dissatisfaction, complaining, self-pity or having a victim complex, was one of the eight deadly traits that the fourth-century desert Christians identified. They spent their lives practising exercises that would overcome these obstacles to the coming of God among them. Psalm 144:14 prays that there may be no complaining in our streets. Absence of complaining makes room for something positive to be experienced.

The trouble with a culture of grumbling is that we don't pay attention to something wonderful. We don't notice potential. We miss the moment.

---

3. See Dale Carnegie, *How to Stop Worrying and Start Living*, Pocket Books, 1990.

Things pile up.
Plenty of noises off.
Grudges cloud the eyes.
The treadmill grinds on,
unless I jump off it into adverts.
Or there is the sacrament of the present moment?

Bible reading
Philippians 2:14, 15

Breathe deeply, rhythmically. Let complaints drain away.
Become aware of the joy in the present moment.

Prayer
Instead of grumbling let there be gratitude,
instead of complaining let there be celebration,
so may there arise a sweet-smelling aroma
that heralds a banquet for a long-awaited guest.

4. Fear

Fear is an emotion aroused by impending danger, evil, pain, or challenge, whether the threat is real or imagined. Fear may be a useful temporary emotion if it warns us of danger, but if we become a prisoner to fear we are lost. Fear of people lest they dominate us, fear of change lest it unsettles us, fear of God lest he reveals uncomfortable truth to us – all such fears prevent what is meant to be from coming into our lives.

'The only thing we have to fear is fear itself.'
Franklin D. Roosevelt

A world business coach gave three apprentices a lump sum of money and asked them to do the best they could with it. The first invested it in a volatile fund with the highest return because her research revealed that market trends were favourable. The second invested it in a long-established fund with a solid, though unspectacular, record of dividends. The third was frightened by the fast-changing nature of the markets. So he hid it in a safe place. At least, he thought, I will not lose it. When the coach arrived to appraise their performance, he affirmed the first two for doing the best they could, according to their lights. But he rebuked the third because, through fear, he had abdicated responsibility for doing the best with what was entrusted to him. 'The one who has nothing will have even that taken from them,' the coach informed the third apprentice.

Fear paralyses. When we are afraid we put down the shutters. This prevents people, good and God from coming in, moving around and doing their work.

People who have given themselves over to the will of God have no fear even of death; they have excised their own will. They are free to do anything on earth and to see God in heaven. Jesus says to us: 'Do not be afraid, little flock, for it is your Father's good pleasure to give you the kingdom' (Luke 12:32).

Bible reading
Matthew 25:14-30

Prayer
Child of Glory, Child of Mary,
at your birth you were proclaimed the Prince of Peace.
You come to remove the wall
that divides one people from another:
may walls of hostility and fear come tumbling down.
May we be alert, active and ready to prepare the way for you.

5. Prejudice

If we don't like immigrants, or westerners, or fashion models, it is unlikely we will discern the face of Jesus in the face of an immigrant, westerner or fashion model. If we belittle the people whose political or moral or religious beliefs clash with ours, we are unlikely to discern the face of Christ in them. We put up a barrier which hinders Christ coming among us.

Sceptics say 'Seeing is believing', yet often we cannot see what we don't want to see. We look for things that confirm our bias and overlook things that don't fit with our bias. We 'see' based on assumptions about how things work. We tend not to see things we do not like or believe in. We filter everything through the lens of 'the script' written for us or by us – a script shaped by our conditioning, culture and values.

Seeing is to some extent a skill we can learn. We can take seriously different perspectives. We can seek opportunities to learn and understand other points of view. We can try to tune in to the feelings of people who are unlike us. In *Mister God, This Is Anna,* Fynn says: 'The sun is nice but it lights things up so much that you can't see very far . . . The night time is better. It stretches your soul to the stars.'[4] Let us use this time of Advent darkness to look long enough at people, to stretch beyond prejudice until we see stardust in them.

Prejudice is closely linked to self-righteousness.
Self-righteousness limits movement and new growth.
It hardens the surfaces of things so that flowers can't shoot up.
It stifles beauty.
It makes the world boring.

---

4. Fynn (pseudonym of Sydney Hopkins), *Mister God, This Is Anna,* Collins, 1974.

Bible reading
Matthew 7:2-4

Prayer
We wait in the darkness, expectantly, longingly.
Help us to see the splendour of the universe –
blankets of stars, the solitary glowing of the planets.
Here below, help us to see stars in the face of a homeless family
and of a person we have written off.

6. Clutter

When rubbish piles up, the Coming gets postponed. When rubbish piles up, spaces can't be used for better purposes. That is why, for material things, we have waste disposal systems. There are also waste disposal systems for interior clutter. For these to achieve their aim, we have first to admit to the clutter and then to dispose of it.

People who go on management courses are familiar with the 'Too Much Stuff To Do – Urgh!' plan: ditch what is unnecessary; delegate what is necessary but which someone else can do; defer (with a timetable) what can wait. For what remains – Do it Now or at the first opportunity.

That is about clearing actions. What about clearing our thoughts and emotions? If I am fixated by my hurts, self-pity or anger, the space in which God can move is already occupied. Have a chat with these fixations: move over a little please; make way for Jesus . . . As you speak these words, imagine how God fills the space you have vacated.

Simplicity is about conscious acts of detachment from hidden bonds that enslave us, about being so detached from self-will that we become free to be the person God created us to be. We do not detach ourselves from love of God or people, but from false substitutes for that love.

What is the excess baggage that we need to be rid of? In the silence, think about, and perhaps jot down, any verbiage transmitted, any items piled up, any duty undertaken through fear of being overlooked – anything that clutters your spirit. Many of us tend to want 'fingers in every pie'. What pies do you wish to have fingers in? Are you free within yourself to let any of these go? In the silence, ask the Holy Spirit to show you.

Bible reading
Matthew 6:28-33

We buy clothes for this and that occasion and soon they clutter our rooms. Jesus suggests that if we live without clutter we have a greater beauty – like the things of nature whose beauty is not hidden by artificial overlays.

Prayer
Your world is becoming a giant rubbish dump.
Spur us to clear out the clutter in our lives, homes and cities until there is space for you to come to your own.

7. Dishonesty

Dishonesty takes a thousand forms, all of which prevent God from coming among us: lies, half-truths, collusion, posturing, cheating, false claims, bribery, manipulation, embezzlement, 'lifting' material from the internet without attribution, embellishments, failure to speak up, pretence, disparagement, gossip . . . you name it.

When we are dishonest, we hide something, we keep things in the dark, the Light is banished. When we spread transparency, the opposite dynamic is released. In 1993, a few individuals decided to take a stand against corruption and created Transparency International. Now present in more than 100 countries, the movement works relentlessly to stir the world's collective conscience and bring about change. It names and shames corrupt business leaders. It has influenced national elections where corruption has threatened to distort the democratic process. It has promoted codes of conduct so that companies can be held accountable for their behaviour, both at home and abroad.

The Advent Hope is that ultimately all will be scrutinised and held to account by the Divine Justice Restorer.

John the Baptist challenged revenue collectors to take only what was due; he challenged the military not to make false charges or take bribes; he challenged believers not to live false lives under a façade of being Abraham's children; he challenged a ruler not to steal his brother's wife; and he challenged everyone to share clothes or food if they met someone who lacked these. No bullying. No bribes. No bamboozlement. These are examples of how to prepare a way for the Lord.

We may ask ourselves: am I honest in my speaking, in the claims I make, in the records I keep?

Bible reading
Luke 3:1-14

Prayer
Among the powerful,
among the spoilt,
among the crooked,
come to make things new.
In halls of fame,
in corridors of power,
in forgotten places,
come to make things new.
With piercing eyes,
with tender touch,
with cleansing love,
come to make things new.

8. Blame

A bad workman blames his tools. Prisoners blame society. Children blame their parents. Citizens blame the government. Governments blame the Opposition. Bad nations blame one another. The USA called Iran part of the 'Axis of Evil' and Iran called USA 'The Great Satan'.

We live in a culture of blame. Reputations are destroyed on Twitter. Trial by media destroys public and private figures. Newspapers feed a 'them and us' mentality. A culture of blame leads to an unwillingness to take risks or to accept responsibility for mistakes, due to fear of criticism or prosecution. A culture of blame erodes trust, sours relationships, limits horizons and undermines teamwork.

How may we clear out a thousand blames that pile up and block the way to God? The spirit of blame is rooted in the false ego that says: 'I am right; you are wrong'.

Bible reading
Genesis 3:12-24

The man blamed the woman for giving him the fruit. The woman blamed the serpent for what today we might call false advertising. The result of the dynamic of blame was loss of trust and walls of separation even within creation and within families, with the resultant pain in child bearing. This is sometimes known as 'the curse of Eve'. Mary, the mother of Jesus, became known as the Second Eve, because she broke the chain of cause and effect. She lived as Eve did before she fell into the blame culture. Breaking the blame chain is essential to the Coming.

Among the Celi De (Friends of God) monks and nuns of eighth-century Ireland, daily confession was as normal and useful as sweeping the floor. Correction 'without harshness, and without blame, and with laughter' was the aim, rather than reproof. Let us ask the Holy Spirit to put her/his finger on the places of blame in our hearts, leave them behind, and be led laughing, hand in hand with God, towards a fresh Coming.

Prayer

Grant us
pain without bitterness,
loss without blame,
forgiveness without remorse,
renewal of trust without fear
that, freed from these burdens,
we may be part of a fresh Coming.

9. Mindlessness

We'd like to clear a way for God to move among us, yet all too often our mindless egos litter the world with stumbling blocks. Examples of mindlessness are:

A mad bull in a china shop
A parent who gets drunk while the baby cries for milk
A mouth that speaks before it thinks
Workers who do endless tasks, oblivious of the needs of those around them
A helper who makes a mess and does not clean it up
A resident who violates the space of neighbours with excessive noise
A fool who rushes in where angels fear to tread.

Mindlessness can be defined as behaving with a lack of attentiveness, awareness or concern for the effects of our actions on other people; a failure to think, feel, or respond appropriately; inertia, a closed heart, or sloppy workflow.

The Lord appeared to Abraham by the oak trees as he sat at the door of his tent in the heat of the day. He noticed three men standing in front of him, ran to greet them, and invited them to take refreshment (Genesis 18:1-33). In the middle of the day we tend to get frazzled. We may either doze off or force ourselves into overdrive. Either way, we tread on other people's toes. We cease to care about anyone else. Abraham, however, was mindful. He noticed travellers. He greeted them. He gave them hospitality. Commenting on this passage, the writer to the Hebrews urges Christians not to forget to practise hospitality for, in doing so, many have entertained angels without realising it (Hebrews 13:2).

Bible reading
Matthew 25:1-13

Father Seraphim taught that the oil in the lamps of the mindful bridesmaids was the Holy Spirit. The Christ is among us when we are mindful to replenish the oil God provides for good living. How may we become mindful? Breathe deeply and be attentive to our breath and body rhythms. Be attentive to the present moment. Be attentive to what and who is around us. Become aware of Who is most deeply within us. Live the moment. In that moment, God comes.

Prayer
Make me attentive to the clouds in the sky,
make me attentive to the soul's every sigh.
Make me aware of the whole and the part,
make me aware of what's in your heart.

10. Things

A king cannot arrive if the route by which he travels is piled with things. Christians, as well as Buddhists, teach the value of detachment. For Buddhists, attachment is the origin, the root and the cause of suffering, because it fails to realise that all is impermanent. Christians teach that detachment from things and union with God is the ultimate goal. Detachment does not mean that we cannot delight in things as gifts, but attachment to anything less than God – such as the fruit of the Tree in the Garden of Eden – is the source of separation from God.

I know a Christian leader who was told that everything he had done, taught and written was a false construct, born of arrogance, which had caused nothing but harm. The accused became ill. He asked himself: 'Should I answer back, draw attention to good fruits, or use this accusation as a spur to practise detachment?' He sat by a holy well at a pilgrim site. First, he made acts of detachment from all merely human constructs he could think of, and mentally threw these into the well. Then he made acts of detachment from everything he had spoken, written or achieved, and threw these into the well. Other things had to follow: the immature ego, childhood conditioning, hopes and fears – they all went into the well. What was left? Nothing – except the joy of Being in the present moment. Just before he rose to leave the well, all kinds of fresh possibilities flooded into his mind. A Buddhist might say that the experiment was a failure, because this man must have become attached to 'possibilities'. But the Advent Hope is that nothingness prepares the way for the only true Reality.

Imagine that Charlie Jones the road-block clearer comes to a briefing meeting. 'Learn to be still,' says the coach. First, the participants turn off their apps and radios. They remove their mobile phones. Then Charlie's mind fills up with things he wants to do. He lets these go until after the meeting. Then his mind fills up with pleasures he looks forward to. He ditches these. Then he focuses on a grievance, an ambition and a lust. On it goes. Eventually he pays attention to the in and out of his breathing. A voice says: 'Out of the Silence leapt the Word.' The coach, as if she had some invisibility wand, says: 'The road is ready. Now stand on guard.'

Bible reading
Colossians 2:5-11

Prayer
The dearest idol I have known,
Whate'er that idol be,
Help me to tear it from Thy throne
And worship only Thee.[5]

---

5. From William Cowper's hymn, *O for a closer walk with God*, 1772.

DECADE TWO
Signposts to the Coming

1. Collapse

The phrase 'This is the Way' often occurs in Scripture. In our second decade of reflections, we imagine ten signposts that we encounter along the Advent Road. The first has these words: 'This road has collapsed – take an alternative route.'

'Things fall apart, the centre cannot hold' wrote the poet W. B. Yeats in The Second Coming. The Christian vision, however, is that God can only fully come when our world does fall apart. Jesus warned that even seemingly stable features such as the sun and moon will dissolve.

When life is smooth, we assume that the familiar landmarks we take for granted will never change. In fact, when familiar human frameworks crumble – family, work, freedom, health, money – the centre we have made for ourselves cannot hold. This gives God a chance, for we will not find the road less travelled if we won't leave the road well travelled. The collapse gives God a chance to work through our vulnerability.

Perhaps we have experienced the limitations which make up the fragments of our lives. 'The hope I have,' someone said, referring to the woman who anointed Jesus by breaking the vase in which was contained the oil, 'is the broken vase from which the oil of anointing comes.' This reminds me of the words of the Apostle Paul that divine treasure comes through our faulty human frames, or as David Adam expressed it in a sermon: 'God uses crack-pots'. Increasing numbers of people now see that the ego-centred world is falling apart and has no future.

Bible reading
Luke 21:25-28

Jesus points out that dissolution is inevitable in some form. We all disintegrate. We all die. But, he tells us, that is not a disaster – it is an opportunity for something divine to be born among us. All eyes shall see him. Do not become drowsy from too much drink or worry. Stand erect. Raise your hands. Be ready.

Prayer
Through the holes let the healing come.
Through the tears let the glory shine.
Through the dyings let the birthings come.
Through the loss let the love flow in.

2. Cleansing

The second sign we notice, on our alternative route, is
'Pilgrims' Wash Rooms'. Before citizens can have a royal
audience, they wash and dress with great care. Christians,
Jews and Muslims – the Children of Abraham – believe
that cleansing is necessary before they can approach God.
A pilgrim told me he had used his days on Holy Island to
make acts of cleansing and sweet offerings of worship inspired
by the framework of the Tabernacle.

In the time of Moses, the people understood that no one
could approach God except Moses himself. Then a portable
tabernacle was created with an outer and inner section. In
the very centre was the Holy of Holies which only the high
priest could enter once a year. This had a mysterious name
that both beckoned and cautioned – 'The Tent of Meeting'.
No one could just wander in even to the outer courtyard.
This had just one entrance. Before they could go through
this, they had to go through a serious process of preparation.
This involved cleansing rituals and offerings.

A bronze altar was set up in front of the entrance in the
courtyard. Every bit of this and the furniture had to be
consecrated to God with anointing oil. The tribe of Aaron
were chosen to service the altar. First, they had to wash
themselves, put on special robes, and consecrate themselves
to the Lord. The covenant, which we know as the Ten
Commandments, inscribed on a tablet, was placed in the
Tent of Meeting. Before it a golden altar was placed. On
this incense was offered. Then, and only then, did the Glory
of the Lord fill the Tent. This was known as the Shekinah
Glory, the very presence of the Lord revealed through sight,
scent and inner sensing. It would come down like a funnel
through the Holy of Holies.

A spirituality has developed based on the Shekinah Glory. Two ministers at Los Angeles' Pentecostal Church on the Way decided to worship in their sanctuary every Saturday evening and pray for those who would gather next day for Sunday worship.

One day, as they fasted and praised God, the whole building was filled with something that looked like golden smoke. Next day, the size of the congregation inexplicably doubled, and God visited that church.

Let us lay down our pride and things we cling to, make offerings of gratitude, and sense the Shekinah Glory, the Divine Presence, in our midst.

Bible reading
Hebrews 10:19-25

Prayer
Search me, O God, and know my heart today,
try me, O Lord, and know my thoughts, I pray;
see if there be some wicked way in me;
cleanse me from every sin, and set me free.[6]

---

6. From a hymn by J. Edwin Orr.

3. Contemplation

The next signpost is to the watch tower. In a bird hide, we need patience and keen eyes, or binoculars to see beyond the obvious. It is like that with God things.

If we are always speaking and never listen, we don't allow time and space for what God may want to say to us. Also, we cannot rush into God's presence. If we keep rushing, we also keep the gulf between us and God. It's like a vicious circle. Contemplatives, however, get foreshadowings of the Word that leaps out of the silence. For the silence is not an absence of something but a presence. At the heart of the silence is he who is all stillness. 'Out of the silence leapt the Word.'[7]

Moses saw a burning bush and knew that he was on holy ground. Isaiah saw the Lord sitting in the temple. He had a vision of a lion lying down with a lamb and a little child leading them. Shepherds who forsook the frenzied pleasures of the town below for the silent watching of sheep in the Bethlehem hills saw a light and heard heavenly sounds.

> At the still point of the turning world
> the business people and the busy people missed it all.
> Only those who had space within
> for liminal knowing
> were drawn to that point.
> They were not taught the point.
> They had no map.
> But they saw, and heard, and came.

---

7. From a traditional Christmas liturgy.

Heaven lies about us in our infancy!
Shades of the prison-house begin to close
Upon the growing Boy,
But he beholds the light, and whence it flows,
He sees it in his joy;
The Youth, who daily farther from the east
Must travel, still is Nature's priest,
And by the vision splendid
Is on his way attended.[8]

Bible reading

Psalm 1:1-3

Prayer

We weave this day silence of knowing,
clearness of seeing, grace of speaking.
We weave this day peace of being,
gift of loving, power of meeting.

---

8. From *Ode to immortality* by William Wordsworth.

4. Creation

The fourth signpost is to a Nature Reserve. It is a reconstruction of various seminal places where creation has revealed God. The river in the Garden of Eden, a peaceful and secluded place, beckons a visitor to take off their clothes, leave behind their excess baggage and walk in the cool of the evening with divine whispers in their ears. From this the visitor emerges into a hard, desert place where she is thirsty and preoccupied with survival. However, a bush keeps burning without being consumed, and a voice says: 'Take off your shoes, for you stand on holy ground.' 'Who are you?' the visitor asks the voice. 'I am what I am and I will be who I will be' comes the reply. Her tribal god, her limiting frameworks, begin to fall away before a greater Reality.

The visitor comes to some trees. One of them, a plaque informs her, is where a certain Brother Lawrence gazed at the tree and was converted to Christ. Further on, a barren fig tree had these words of Jesus fixed to it: 'May you never bear fruit again.'

Bible reading
Mark 11:12-14, 20-26

Bible commentators suggest that Jesus' cursing of the barren fig tree was a prophetic sign that the period of the Jews as the main fruitful agency of God on earth was coming to an end. However, if any of his followers prayed with faith, they could see miracles on earth. There is a relationship between the Creator and creation. Creation linked to human faith can be a sign that we can expect something more from God.

God revealed himself to Moses through a bush, to Jeremiah through an almond tree and to magi through a star. Contemplate the air of the eternal seeping through the physical, and the glory of God peeping through the cosmos.

Question: What is the fruit of study?

Answer: To perceive the eternal Word of God reflected in every plant and insect, every bird and animal, and every man and woman.

Early British catechism

Look for signs of the Coming in the sacrament of creation.

Prayer

You are the Rock from which all earth is fashioned.
You are the Food from which all souls are fed.
You are the Force from which all power lines travel.
You are the Source – by you we shall be led.

5. Family Trees

A surprising signpost to the 'Family Ancestry Research Centre' appears. The opening room asks the question: 'Are there DNA patterns from the past that offer a clue to our future?' The central room focuses on Jesus' family tree. In the window is a Jesse Tree. Jesse was the father of King David who was an ancestor of both Jesus' mother and his father. Jesus has been called 'Great David's greater Son'. Jesse Trees like this appear in churches and homes in many places during Advent. Children draw symbols of one of Jesus' ancestors on a card and hang these on the tree. There may be symbols of wisdom, justice and service.

Bible reading
1 Samuel 16:1-13

It was the way David was chosen as king that holds a clue to a way in which God can break through our closed systems. Following a failed experiment in kingship, God told the seer Samuel to meet the sterling farmer and landowner named Jesse and interview his strapping sons, with a view that he would before long put one of them forward to be anointed as the new king. These young men were strong, hard-working, honest, able and good-looking. Yet no inner conviction accompanied the interviews that 'this was the one'. So Samuel asked if there was any other son who had been missed out. There was. He was the youngster David who was out in the fields, looking after sheep. He had been ruled out because, as the youngest, he could do less and they took him for granted. Samuel called for him, looked on his heart and saw that David had a heart for God. He had the right attitudes. He was eager, loyal, supple, quick to learn. Jesse may have overlooked his youngest son's hidden qualities and his potential, but God did not, and neither did Samuel.

Visualise Jesse's family tree as a physical tree in your landscape. Then visualise a branch shooting out. In order to grow more spiritually aware, review the way you make decisions and the parameters you take for granted. Become aware of how incomplete and sometimes inaccurate your information is. Instead of rushing ahead, allow your deeper senses and intuitions to inform you. When we do these things, we become open to a new direction or a surprising impulse. In such ways, Emmanuel comes to us.

Prayer
Come to us
in the innocent person in the background,
in the person of integrity who seeks no limelight,
in the eager face and laugh of an untarnished human being,
in the person after your own heart.

6. Runners

The next signpost says 'Look out for runners'. Motorists are often given such warnings when there is a fun run or marathon through town streets. To herald a forthcoming Olympic Games, people run with the Olympic flame across the world. I met some of these chosen runners when the Olympic Games came to the UK in 2012. These runners were not what I had expected. These Olympic heralds were chosen for their good works, or because they had a disability which they had overcome, and not only for their athletic prowess.

The start of Jesus of Nazareth's local campaign with a global outreach was heralded by his cousin John. In the West he is known as John the Baptist but in the East he is known as John the Forerunner. In the spirit of the prophets Elijah and Isaiah, he ran ahead to prepare the way of the Lord.

In what ways was John a runner? He came out of the desert and excited crowds of Jews who wanted a decent, God-led world with the anticipation of a Messianic figure. He called them to prepare by practising good works and restorative justice and by being washed (baptised) in the river Jordan.

There are famous stories in ancient societies of runners completing long distances in order to bring a king news of a victory or defeat. The story of the first marathon runner is legendary. Philippides, the courier, brought the news of victory in the Battle of Marathon to Athens and addressed the magistrates there in session when they were anxious how the battle had ended: 'Joy to you, we've won,' he said, and there and then he died, breathing his last breath with the words 'Joy to you'.

Somebody who is nimble and fit for purpose elicits our attention. If they are like one of those runners who carry the flame that heralds the coming of the Olympic Games, we become aware that something worthwhile is drawing near. There are spiritual equivalents to such runners. They are sometimes called Athletes of the Spirit. These are people who are in the right place at the right time with the right attitude. 'Bingo,' we say because that is a winning combination. 'Bingo,' we say, because there is something in the air.

This idea that when the world or the Church sinks into bad ways runners arrive who live the disciplines and excite appetites for a new way of God became a pattern. The fourth-century desert fathers and mothers were known as Christ's Athletes. A thousand years later, similar Athletes of Christ emerged in the forests of Russia. Who are the physical or spiritual runners in our society? Where are the God-stirrings? Seek them out. Become part of them. See what God will do.

Bible reading
Mark 1:1-8

Prayer
All-holy God, front runners like John clear obstacles from your path and point their finger to your hot spots. Help us to run the way of your commands, and to run with a vision so clear that passers-by can get it.

7. Angels

A signpost to 'Angel Hill' leads into a slip road. The visitor then ascends the hill.

Those who drive from London to Edinburgh on the A1 road are familiar with the Angel of the North. This huge structure overlooks England's industrial north-east. It is not ephemeral. It is solid, gritty, and looks as if it is made from the iron of an aircraft hangar. The thing about angels is that they are not what you expect.

Jacob saw angels go up and down on a ladder which reached from the place where he had dossed down for the night and up into heaven. Jacob's progeny divided into two kingdoms. As he died, he pronounced that a sceptre would come from his son Judah. Bible texts suggest this prophecy was fulfilled in the birth of the Christ. Jacob was not a 'good' man, but he was a determined man. Emmanuel can come to difficult persons who want God's will above all things.

In Nazareth, Joseph discovered his teenage fiancée was pregnant, but not by him, and he intended to put her away. An angel came to him in a night vision and assured him the child was from God. Angel intimations don't fit into our nice formulas and correct theologies. The girl, Mary, had neither status nor public relations behind her. An angel told her she would have a child. She could not make it out, but she said yes to it. Saying yes to something deeper than logic, that we somehow know is meant to be, makes room for God to come in a way he has never come before.

An example from the early history of Britain is of a bishop in the kingdom of Kent. A pagan king had replaced his Christian predecessor and the bishop planned to flee for his life. But in the night an angel slapped him hard and told him to stay. When he showed the king his wounds, the king converted to Christ and the Kent mission was saved.

During meditation, someone sensed God saying: 'You do well to remember your unseen friends. Companying with them, the more you live in this Unseen World the less earth's troubles will overwhelm you and the gentler will be your passing when it comes.'

Bible reading
Matthew 1:18-25

Prayer
O kindly angels of God, attend to us this night.
Rescue us in the battling floods;
clothe us, for we are naked;
succour us, for we are feeble and forlorn;
steer our vessels in the tempests of life.
Guide our step in gap and in pit;
guard us in the treacherous turnings
and save us from the harm any wish upon us.[9]

---

9. Echoes *Carmina Gadelica.*

8. Little Things

The next signpost seems rather insignificant and a bit of a mystery. It directs the traveller to an accommodation centre named 'The House of Little Things'. Thimbles, pins, mirrors, dog brushes, kettles, tissues and aspirins grace the shelves and there are foot rests in front of the armchairs.

It reminds us of the Bible verse: 'Do not despise these small beginnings'.[10] Wales' patron saint David is reputed to have said to his brothers before he died: 'Do the little things, the small things you've seen me doing.' Archbishop Rowan Williams thinks that phrase resonates with modern people because 'it reminds us that the primary things for us are the relationships around us, the need to work at what's under our hands, what's "within our reach". We can transform our domestic, our family relationships, our national life to some extent, if we do that with focus and concentration in the presence of God.'

I come in the little things,
Saith the Lord:
Yea! On the glancing wings
Of eager birds, the softly pattering feet
Of furred and gentle beasts, I come to meet
Your hard and wayward heart. In brown bright eyes
That peep from out the brake, I stand confessed.
On every nest
Where feathery Patience is content to brood
And leaves her pleasure for the high emprize
Of motherhood –
There doth My Godhead rest.

---

10. Zechariah 4:10 [New Living Translation]

I come in the little things,
Saith the Lord:
My starry wings
I do forsake,
Love's highway of humility to take:
Meekly I fit My stature to your need.
In beggar's part
About your gates I shall not cease to plead –
As man, to speak with man –
Till by such art
I shall achieve My Immemorial Plan,
Pass the low lintel of the human heart.[11]

Bible Reading
Zechariah 4:10

Prayer
In the little things we do,
be present, Lord.
In the little things we speak,
be present, Lord.
In the little moments we fill,
be present, Lord.

---

11. From Evelyn Underhill, *Immanence*, in Nicholson & Lee, eds., *The Oxford Book of English Mystical Verse*, 1917.

9. Donkey World

The ninth signpost is to 'Donkey World'. How strange! What have donkeys to do with our coming destiny or with any of the models of world government that compete for our allegiance?

ISIS-type groups attract recruits from numerous countries. These recruits, like many others who stay at home, feel they don't fit in the world as it is. They are angry. The idea of giving everything, even their lives, for a caliphate under God attracts them. This is how they think God is coming on earth.

They are critical of capitalism, although they may take its benefits for granted. But capitalism has blessings as well as sins. The target should be its sins. The free market enables the needs of the world to be met. Food, water, houses, transport, shops, infrastructures, education, health, power supplies – all these are engineered, created, distributed and improved because competition keeps quality up, changing needs identified, systems efficient, prices down. The sins of capitalism are putting money and success above community, trust, honesty, the poor. If the free market is replaced by state socialism, the sins of inertia and selfishness lead to breakdown of services, poor quality of goods, and dependency.

So the idea of replacing capitalism or communism with a society ruled by God-proclaimers is appealing. At various times it has been tried by Jews, Christians and Muslims, but it has never worked. Why? Because power corrupts even religious leaders, and because the sins that are endemic in human nature remain as bad as ever.

The Bible gives us clues to an alternative basis for true government. Donkeys are one clue.

Bible reading

Rejoice greatly . . . Lo, your king comes to you; triumphant and victorious is he, humble and riding on a donkey, on a colt, the foal of a donkey . . . he shall command peace to the nations (Zechariah 9:9, 10).

The prophet of one country signposts a king who will bring peace to all countries. Unlike kings the world has so far known, this one will be humble and will ride, not on spectacular crowd-pulling transport, but upon the most menial of beasts.

Jesus was carried in a womb bumped along the road to Bethlehem by a donkey. At the end of his physical life, which presaged the beginning of his unseen pilot reign, he rode into the capital city on a donkey colt to fulfil Zechariah's prophecy.

Meditate on this: If we start at the bottom we can only rise. If we start at the top we can only fall.

Prayer

Little donkey, carry us beyond Bethlehem,
through refugee camps and killing fields to the place where everyone shines.

10. Births

The tenth signpost simply says 'Pregnancy Clinic'. This has a research department which unearths facts about some of history's most extraordinary births. There is Sarah, who was long past child-bearing age, yet God promised her husband Abraham that he would become the father of more people than there are grains of sand. At first it seemed that prophecy came true through his slave woman who gave birth to Ishmael. Then, against all the odds, Sarah herself gave birth to Isaac. There is Hannah. The old man at the local shrine thought she was drunk, but in fact this infertile woman was pouring out her agonies of longing to God. Her lips moved but no sounds came out. No wonder he thought she was drunk. She told God that if he gave her a child she would dedicate its life to his service. She gave birth to Samuel, who learned to listen to God at a time when the art of listening had been lost. He became a seer and king maker. Another woman highlighted by the clinic is Elizabeth, another no-hoper, who gave birth to John the Baptist.

Then there are newspaper articles about virgin births in nature and the possibilities of a human virgin birth. There is an account of Mary of Bethlehem who gave birth to Jesus. There is even a section on 'male pregnancies'. Scientists mean different things by this phrase, but there is no doubt that men 'give birth' to ideas, art, compassionate projects and movements of human fellowship.

Glimpses of God's plan were given when Columba's birth was foretold to elders of Ireland in visions and dreams. Columba's mother Eithne dreamed she was given a great cloak that stretched from Ireland to Scotland and contained every colour of the rainbow. A youth took this radiant cloak from her, which made her extremely sad. Then the youth returned to Eithne and said, 'You have no need of grief but rather of joy and delight. The meaning of this dream is that you will bear a son, and Ireland and Scotland will be full of his teaching.' Each of us is formed in the imagination of God. Let us interrupt life's treadmill and live what we are created to be.

Bible reading
Luke 1:5-25

The Christ is born anew whenever we become receptacles of the Holy Spirit.

Christ comes in those who say 'Yes'. Let us say 'yes' with all our being.

Prayer
Holy God, holy and mighty,
you can bring a holy child to birth in a barren womb,
you can bring a new thing to birth in a barren land.
Bring to birth in me that new thing that is your will.

DECADE THREE

Make ready for the Coming

1. Welcome Wisdom

Road blocks to the Coming have been cleared, though road clearance must remain a life-long habit. Signs have helped us be in the right place. Now, we must prepare an environment fit for a king. If a space is created but is not filled with a welcome for goodness, seven devils may fill it. So we begin ten days when we make a welcome for the King of kings to come among us.

In Christian tradition, a prayer response called an antiphon is said every day from 17 December until Christmas Eve. Each prayer is addressed to God under a title for the Messiah referred to in a prophecy of Isaiah. By the eighth century, these prayer responses were used quite widely. Roman Catholics have seven, Anglicans added another. Today we add further ones, including those awakened in us through contemplation of God in creation.

These antiphons were instituted in the days when Latin was the language of liturgy. The antiphon for 17 December is O Sapientia. In English the phrase 'Come, O Wisdom from on high' is used.

Later some Benedictines played around with these Latin titles and formed an acrostic.

If one starts with the last title and takes the first letter of each one – **E**mmanuel, **R**ex, **O**riens, **C**lavis, **R**adix, **A**donai, **S**apientia – the Latin words **ero cras** are formed, meaning 'Tomorrow, I will come'. Therefore, the Lord Jesus, whose coming we have prepared for in Advent and whom we address in these seven Messianic titles, now says to us, 'Tomorrow, I will come.' So the O Antiphons not only bring intensity to our Advent preparation, but bring it to a joyful conclusion.

Bible reading
Isaiah 11:1-3

Today we invite the Wisdom from on high to grow in us. If we are 'in Christ', how may we grow in wisdom? Reflect upon each element of the following sentence:

> Wisdom begins with reverence for God, comes into focus when we know our place, forms when we observe, strengthens when we exercise restraint, matures when we look at both sides of an issue, broadens when we ask questions, deepens when we resist headstrong ways, thrives when we reflect, flowers when we drink daily from its well-springs.

Prayer
Come to us, Wisdom,
moving in the flux and flow of the cosmos to bring worlds into being.
Come to us, Wisdom,
swirling in the elements and bringing God's Son to earth.
Come to us, Wisdom,
the seeing eye of art and science, the ear of all that breathes.
Come to us, Wisdom,
the weaver of Earth's destiny, the completer of our call.

2. Relish Beauty

Beauty is the radiance of truth; the fragrance of goodness.
Vincent McNabb, Irish scholar and priest, 1868–1943

When Jesus began his public ministry in Galilee, he read in a synagogue from the scroll of the prophet Isaiah some words that were thought to refer to the Messiah. It was a kind of manifesto. It included these words: 'God has anointed me to bestow on them a crown of beauty to replace the ashes worn by mourners.'

In his novel *The Idiot* Dostoevsky wrote: 'Beauty will save the world.' This statement is not idolatrous. He meant, I suspect, that truth, beauty and goodness are three expressions of God and that beauty, unlike the other two, woos us.

In a BBC Radio 4 interview on 27 December 2011, Archbishop Rowan Williams spoke of the powerful sense, in Russian Christianity in particular, 'of the things of this world being shot through with puzzle, beauty, mystery, danger. The liturgy as a great drama – worship as not just addressing a few well-chosen remarks to God but being caught up in something, in the fullest sense, theatrical.'[12]

In my book *Waymarks for the Journey* I wrote: 'We can learn through beauty because God is the Source of beauty, and each glimpse of beauty can become a teacher of our soul, revealing to us some quality of God, wooing us, beckoning us, leading us one more small step into the Mystery of God. Beauty teaches us that production figures and league tables, the mere amassing of data, are not the whole truth about this world or the next. Beauty leads us beyond itself.'[13]

---

12. http://rowanwilliams.archbishopofcanterbury.org/articles.php/2311/archbishop-on-dosto-evsky-radio-4s-one-to-one-programme#sthash.ot0cNpgB.dpuf
13. Ray Simpson, *Waymarks for the Journey*, Kevin Mayhew, 2009.

Today let us reflect on something beautiful or do something beautiful for God. As we open up to beauty, we are allowing the Messiah to come and make this like a crown upon our heads.

Bible reading
Isaiah 61:1-4

Prayer
Divine Source of Beauty,
our minds are like a field.
In this field, please grow many good things,
many true things with deep roots
and many beautiful things,
ever fresh, ever lovely, ever fragrant.

3. Take Delight

A sign that God's kingdom is among us is, according to one Advent psalm, delight: 'you give them drink from the river of your delights' (Psalm 36:8).

One of the Genesis accounts of creation pictures God resting from the work of creating, not because he was tired, but because he wanted time to delight in what he had created (Genesis 1:31–2:3).

The Book of Proverbs pictures Wisdom as a divine Playmate: 'I was daily his delight, rejoicing before him always, rejoicing in his inhabited world and delighting in the human race' (Proverbs 8:30, 31).

We know that Jesus took delight in inviting people to a meal table, and that he described the kingdom of God as a banquet. Theatre Damfino created a participatory 'picnic of the senses' called *The Table of Delights* which included pirouetting beetroots, singing honey bees, flying eggs and a feast of good tales!

Christmas is above all God taking delight in the world he has made. How may we make our Christmas and New Year celebrations tables of delight? The scents of good food? Party poppers? Creative decorations? Poems? Recalling of memories?

> We saw a stranger yesterday.
> We put food in the eating place,
> Drink in the drinking place,
> Music in the listening place.
> And with the sacred name of the triune God
> He blessed us and our house,
> Our cattle and our dear ones.
> As the lark says in her song:

Often, often, often goes the Christ
In the stranger's guise.

A Celtic Rune

Bible reading
Psalm 36:7-9

Prayer
As we share this foretaste of the heavenly feast,
generous be our hearts,
open be our hands,
delight be in our faces,
thanksgiving be our call.

4. Star-gaze – Think Outside the Box

'In the beginning was the Life-Force and the Life-Force was divine . . . and became a human being' (John 1:1, 14[14]). I am no scientist, but as far as I know I have not closed my mind to fresh discoveries. Some new atheists who happen to be scientists seem to have closed minds. I read Richard Dawkins' *The God Delusion*.[15] It showed such ignorance of theology that its author would have failed a GCSE exam in religious studies. We used to hear criticisms that some theologians had put God in a box. Now we hear criticisms that such scientists put science in a box.

My mind is blown, however, by a talk at Glastonbury's Chalice Well Garden on 'The Conscious Universe' by writer John Martineau. He reminds us that we are surrounded by breathtaking eco-systems in an awesome universe. He argues that the role of randomness in evolutional theory is shrinking and that the fast-moving new field of epigenetics suggests other factors are also at play. For example, we now know that parental preferences and patterns get passed down in plants and people. Adaptations in, for example, small cichlid fish trapped in a glacial lake occurred more than ten times faster than they should have by random mutation alone. Something else is going on. Could it, he argues, be mind and imagination? Could the fish be saying 'Jeez, if only I had a little hook on my lip I could get that slime in that crack!'

Another area where randomness is in retreat is morphology – the shapes of things.

Professor Simon Conway Morris of Cambridge University tells us that the camera eye has separately evolved the same mode of perception in octopi, humans and box jellyfish. Does this tell us that it is not random?

---

14. Author's paraphrase.
15. Bantam Books, 2006.

The same thing is true of the whole universe. The part of it we can see is over 90 billion light years across. We don't know what lies beyond. What we do know is that our universe is very life-friendly. Since the 1970s, scientists have calculated that it is optimised for life. Water, nitrogen, carbon and various organic compounds freely form and float around in huge gas clouds in space. The whole place is incredibly finely tuned to optimise the chances for things like us popping up. So how does it get so finely tuned for life? Atheist scientists take a leap of dogmatism, and opine that there must be billions of such universes (a multiverse) so, if one in billions gets the right combination, it is still just an accident. Are there other explanations besides this unprovable fantasy? Oxford University's Nick Bostrom has suggested that the universe may be a huge evolving organism whose optimal tuning is inherited from successful 'parents'. He wonders what it's like outside the box and who built it?

We can best prepare for 'a Coming' by keeping our minds and our hearts open.

Bible reading
John 1:1-14

Prayer
You are the Force from which all power lines travel.
You are the Source from which creation beams.
You are the Heart from which all hearts are beating.
You are the Mind from which come thoughts and dreams.
You are the Eye from which comes all our seeing.
You are the Gift from whom all mercy streams.

5. Create Cribs

About 1223 Saint Francis of Assisi pondered how to make the events of Jesus' birth at Bethlehem come alive for the people of his time. So, near the town of Greccio, he created a crib with live people and animals. This popularised the idea of making a crib scene in homes, churches, schools, shops and town centres at Christmas.

In Krakow, Poland, stone masons began to make cribs during the idle weeks of rainy autumn. This pastime caught on among all kinds of people. Nowadays the city comes alive with ornate portable theatres for Nativity plays. These brightly illuminated extravaganzas are inspired by Krakow's architectural marvels. In addition, every church takes pride in creating its own unique crib scene.

Bethlehem, Jesus' birthplace, hosts the International Nativity Museum on the ground floor of the historic Salesian Convent. This creates a rhapsody of crib customs and spiritualities from around the world. A survey on the museum's website explains baby Jesus' almond eyes and Thailandese dresses and how he is kept warm by llamas. It refers to the poetry of Andine and South American wood-cribs, to the charm of the Asiatic pieces, to the European range in its diversity from rigorous to original pieces, and to how the wooden carved crib from Africa has no end in its power to astonish.

Christmas has been hijacked by secular, hedonistic and money-making people. We may feel powerless against such a tide. We are not powerless. To simply make, display or reflect upon a crib speaks infinitely more than the razzmatazz. Child-like simplicity, connection with animals, the wonder of another dimension speak more than all the advertisements. Let us carry the Christ-Child into the market place.

In the bleak midwinter a stable place sufficed
The Lord God Almighty, Jesus Christ . . .
Enough for him, whom cherubim
Worship night and day,
A breastful of milk,
And a mangerful of hay;
Enough for him, whom angels
Fall down before,
The ox and ass and camel
Which adore.

Christina Rossetti (1830–1894)

Bible reading

Luke 2:8-16

Prayer

It is right that human beings should acknowledge your divinity.
It is right for the heavenly beings to worship your humanity.
For heavenly beings were amazed to see how small you became,
and earthly ones to see how exalted.

Ephrem the Syrian, d. 371

6. Offer Gifts of Kindness

When I was a child, I used to get excited about the coming of Father Christmas. He always left me presents. I said, 'Mummy, won't he get hungry? Can I leave him something?' We left him a saucer of milk. The following year my big brother said, 'There is no Father Christmas. It's our parents who leave the presents. I can prove it. They are stacked at the top of the wardrobe in their bedroom.' I was shocked, disappointed, but not destroyed, for the fiction of Santa Claus was replaced by the fact of two loving parents who cared enough to give presents, even though they would not be thanked.

My Bible class teachers said, 'Don't worry, the best Christmas present of all is Jesus.' Although Jesus came in human form, he is Spirit. He can come down the chimney and into our bedroom at any time, though he tends to respect boundaries; he needs us to invite him. It would, however, be extremely ungracious if we did not give to Jesus in return.

> What can I give him, poor as I am?
> If I were a shepherd, I would give a lamb.
> If I were a wise man, I would do my part.
> Yet what I can I give him – give my heart.
> *Christina Rossetti*

The most lovely gifts are acts of kindness. In Iran, people create 'walls of kindness' as part of an outdoor charity initiative in which strangers leave goods they no longer require for those who need them. Coats, jackets, boots hang from hooks fixed to these walls, which are sometimes protected by a plastic covering. In a century struck by brutality and indifference, kindness makes its appearance in the streets.

I would prepare a feast and be host to the great High King,
with all the company of heaven.
The sustenance of pure love be in my house,
the roots of repentance in my house.
Baskets of love be mine to give,
with cups of mercy for all the company.

Traditional – sometimes attributed to St Brigid

Bible reading

Matthew 25:31-40

Prayer

Divine Christmas Gift, renew in us the gift of friendship
and the gift of kindness,
the gift of sharing and the gift of love.

7. Make Room

For nine months he who is angels' Lord
was hidden, love's furnace, in a little room,
humbler than all, whom all adored.
A pure lamb, he stole down to earth
to free us from our sin so blind.
No city home will shield his birth,
his mother a stable for bed must find.
Tadg Gaelach O Suilleabhain (1715–95)

A house is a physical structure. In contrast, a home, according to one dictionary, is 'an environment offering security and happiness . . . a valued place regarded as a refuge or place of origin'.

A greater number of people than ever before choose the single life or live alone. Home life, in secular western societies, rarely consists of an extended family. Yet that does not invalidate the principle that each human being has a choice, to make a home for the One who longs to come to his own, or to shut him out.

God has many names that place him higher than all. The name Emmanuel, however, places God among us, in our homes. It is one of the names given to Jesus (Luke 1:31). It means God With Us.

Jesus is not simply born on earth, he is born in a stable rather than in a palace. But in order for him to be born even in that Bethlehem out-house, someone had to welcome his parents in and make room for him.

It is ever thus. Where people make room for God, he comes to live with them. Each such place becomes an epiphany. In an age when there is more persecution of Christians than ever before, could there also be more little Bethlehems than ever before?

In order for pilgrims to enter Bethlehem's Church of the Nativity they have to bend low at its little door. Wherever we humble ourselves to live in the Defenceless Love of the Babe of Bethlehem, there the Light shines.

Bible reading
Luke 2:1-7

Prayer
Home-maker God, as we look into the face of the babe of Bethlehem, the face of defenceless love, in your mercy look upon your troubled world. Fear and violence, homelessness and pollution, grief and anxiety stalk it. Move the hearts of governments and peoples to use your gifts of wealth and skill to build your kingdom of love, where we shall live free from cruelty, neglect and fear. Free us to see Christ in the face of another person, and to look into the face of everyone with welcome.

8. Develop Spiritual Intelligence

Why did 'simple' people like shepherds become aware that a baby they had not yet seen had special significance, while 'intelligent' hoteliers, who did see the baby, missed the significance? Recent research reveals that there are different kinds of intelligence.

The IQ test, which measures things like linguistic and mathematical intelligence, was invented by Alfred Binet. But we may recall Dustin Hoffman's character Raymond in the film *Rain Man* – he computed endless numbers in his head but did not understand the basics of interpersonal communication. Daniel Goleman and others identified two further expressions of intelligence – emotional and social intelligence.

In 1997 the writer Danah Zohar coined the term 'spiritual intelligence'.[16] She and other writers who explored it identified aspects such as: empathy, being vision- and value-led, living from principles and deep beliefs, seeing larger patterns, relationships, and connections, having a sense of belonging and humility, having the sense of being a player in a larger drama, of one's true place in the world.

In 2012 Cindy Wigglesworth published the results of her researches in a book entitled *SQ21: The Twenty-One Skills of Spiritual Intelligence.*[17] She describes the person of spiritual intelligence as a fully human person with the ability to behave with wisdom and compassion, while maintaining inner and outer peace, regardless of the situation. A spiritually intelligent person has the ability to reframe, makes positive use of adversity and feels called upon to give something back.

---

16. Danah Zohar, *ReWiring the Corporate Brain: Using the New Science to Rethink How We Structure and Lead Organizations,* Berrett-Koehler, 1997.
17. Select Books, New York, 2014.

She drew up a list of 22 skills that we can learn. These include awareness of the false ego and the true self, of our own and others' world views, of spiritual laws and our own blind spots, of one's values and purpose.

These qualities have resonance with those attributed to the Messiah, who is the representative of the Full Human Being. The Christmas message is that the Messiah is now among us, and that it is possible for us all to 'come to ... the knowledge of the Son of God, to maturity, to the measure of the full stature of Christ' (Ephesians 4:13). We can carry the Christ within us and into the world around.

Bible Reading
Isaiah 11:1, 2

Prayer
Glorious Messiah,
whose birth shows us the wonder of being human
and whose glory is seen in human life coming fully alive,
help us to live fully human lives for you in the power of Jesus Christ,
truly human, truly divine.

9. Feast Together

I discovered The Feast in Birmingham, England's second largest and most multi-ethnic city. Young Muslims and Christians gather in friendship for a meal and share something from their faith that inspires them. Muslims honour a list of 99 names of God. Christians delight to recall the many titles of God or the Messiah in the Bible. The Feast, and other multi-faith youth groups, sometimes spend an evening when each person who wishes chooses the name for God that means most to them, and they may explain why. God the All-Merciful often tops the list.

The Feast is a Christian charity, empowering young people to become peacemakers and spearhead social change. They also engage in outdoor, fitness and ecological activities. They have adopted part of the Grand Union Canal.

Hannah Jacobs explained on The Feast's blog how every day of her life since starting secondary school was filled with anxiety for the future. It was as if she was in a box, stuck in an endless nightmare. Then she went to an after-school club run by The Feast. This was like a ray of light in the darkness. She felt a burst of joy surging through her. She knew then that the one thing she could do was to help people. Each day she thought about those in poverty, those who were getting bullied or stressed or who suffered racial abuse or natural disaster. And about the planet being abused. She concluded: 'I want to change the world.'

Bible Reading
Isaiah 7:10-15

People at The Feast reflected on the names of God. Qur'an names for God include: the Protector, the All-Compassionate, the Great Forgiver, the All-seeing, the Provider. A number of names of God appear in both sacred Scriptures, such as the First and the Last. Old Testament names for God include: El Shaddai, the All-Sufficient One (Genesis 17:1); the Lord will Provide (Genesis 22:14); the Lord that Heals (Exodus 15:26); Emmanuel – God With Us (Isaiah 7:14). What a good way to prepare for Christmas.

Prayer

Come, First and Last; Come, Provider; Come, Great Forgiver. Come, Emmanuel.

10. Embrace Birth Pains

Jesus told the 70 witnesses he sent out to prepare the way for him how they could know where to make ready for his coming: wherever they were welcomed. We can prepare for the Coming by taking down the 'keep out' notices which, often unacknowledged by ourselves, we put up whenever we find persons or tasks or ideas that we find inconvenient. There is no birth without birth pains. The welcome requires us to embrace these birth pains.

> God will come like a baby
> After an anxious wait.
> With a gush, a push, a slip and a shout
> he's out.

> She will come like a drought-breaking storm
> With all the drama of a sound and light show,
> Followed by a long soak
> of joy.

> He will come like a breeze
> After a three showers a day scorcher.
> Like the mid-afternoon north-easterly sea breeze
> he comes.

> God will come like a great undoing.
> How could this happen to me?
> I would have preferred my own death
> to this.

Then out of the cracks in the ruins of life
creeps hope.
God will come and she is already here.
This is seen most clearly in retrospect.

Heather Johnston
(Community of Aidan and Hilda,
Buderim, Queensland)

Glow to him, sky and sea.
Glow to him, rock and tree.
Now that the Son of God we see.

Bible Reading
John 15:21-24

Prayer
Through your birth,
teach us the grace of defenceless love.
Through your obedience,
teach us the grace of acceptance.
Through your dying,
teach us the grace of eternal life.

DECADE FOUR
Glimpses of glory

1. Seers

The Epiphany Hope is that the Light shining through Christ spreads to all people and to all areas of life. Sadly, some people say: 'We don't see it.' Today we focus on two people, Anna and Simeon, who did see it. They had a glimpse of present glory in the infant Jesus and of future glory expressed in the transformation of peoples. If we can learn from them a new way of seeing, the Epiphany Hope will be fulfilled. Anna and Simeon were two aged seers. Anna had lived alone most of her life. She prayed in the Jerusalem temple day and night. She had no doubt seen hundreds of babies dedicated to God there. This time she sensed something of a different order. She praised God for this baby and told many people about him.

Anna and Simeon provide windows into the character of faith, which can often be lonely. They sense both the sword and the salvation that Mary will experience. Their rejoicing and encouragement come only after *years* of private waiting. And though history-changing events have begun to unfold, Anna and Simeon teach us that God cares not only about the world, but also about each *one* of us. This is good news for old people. The Spirit of God can rest upon them.

In the Old Testament, seers, though only a tiny minority of the population, could see clearly what was going to happen to a person or a people, because they could see into their spiritual condition, and could discern, through the law of cause and effect, what outcomes their spiritual condition would lead to.

David Adam writes of the Celtic peoples: 'Somehow...due to their history [they] have been able to keep an awareness of the "other" far more easily than most peoples . . . Everything spoke of a Presence, vibrated with his love. They saw a universe ablaze with his glory, suffused with a presence that calls, nods and beckons – a creation personally united with its Creator in every atom and fibre . . . This was expressed in a beautifully simple way by a woman from Kerry in the south west of Ireland. When she was asked where heaven was, she replied: "about a foot and a half above a person". Such an awareness has us always treading exciting border lands . . . We need to regain a sense of wonder, reverence and awe.'

Bible reading
Luke 2:25-40

Prayer
Great Spirit of the seers and sacred words:
come into our minds,
come into our mouths
until we become your presence and sign.

2. The Bright Field

'Christmas lasts for ever' say stickers on car rear windows but, for many, Christmas fades with the last piece of Christmas cake. Yet Christmas does indeed last and grow among those who have eyes to see ever-new glimpses of the Glory:

> I have seen the sun break through
> to illuminate a small field
> for a while, and gone my way
> and forgotten it. But that was the pearl
> of great price, the one field that had
> treasure in it. I realise now
> that I must give all that I have
> to possess it. Life is not hurrying
>
> on to a receding future, nor hankering after
> an imagined past. It is the turning
> aside like Moses to the miracle
> of the lit bush, to a brightness
> that seemed as transitory as your youth
> once, but is the eternity that awaits you.[18]

This poem by the Welsh poet priest, R.S. Thomas, speaks about an epiphany. The poet confides that he has often seen the sun 'illuminate a small field' for a moment, and continued on his way and 'forgotten it'. But, says Thomas, he knows that that field was 'the pearl of great price'; that moment was something rare and beautiful, to hold on to and spend your life searching for. He is admitting here that he has experienced moments of profound connection to God, but that he has proceeded to move on, without dwelling on it. However, he

---

18. In R.S. Thomas, *Collected Poems*, Phoenix Press, 2000.

has now come to realise that he must 'give all that I have/to possess' that moment – that 'bright field' – again.

The second section of the sonnet suggests that another quality of these bright moments of grace are in fact moments where we are intensely *present*, when we are most alive. In this case the image of a bright field brought an epiphany. What bright image comes to your mind? What dimensions of epiphany unfold for you?

Bible reading
Matthew 13:44

To find the treasure, we have to let go of whatever we cling to.

Prayer
God our Treasure,
who showers treasures upon your people,
help us to discover fresh treasure in Scripture and silence, in saints and seasons,
in friendship and in familiar scenes.

3. There's a Light upon the Mountains

There is a place in Kwa Zulu-Natal, South Africa, named The Valley of a Thousand Hills. A canoe marathon is run there every year and Methodists hold a youth camp. A science student went to one of these, though he had little faith. One evening, as they looked out to the hills, everyone sang:

There's a light upon the mountains,
and the day is at the spring,
when our eyes shall see the beauty
and the glory of the King;
weary was our heart with waiting,
and the night-watch seemed so long,
but his triumph-day is breaking,
and we hail it with a song.

He is breaking down the barriers,
He is casting up the way;
He is calling for his angels
to build up the gates of day;
But his angels here are human,
not the shining hosts above,
for the drum-beats of his army
are the heart-beats of our love.

Henry Burton (1840–1930)

That young man was transformed. He saw the light. He is now an Anglican priest.

What was it that brought Christ's transforming light to a non-believer in a valley of a thousand hills? Was it Christ beckoning through the landscape, or signalling his eternal glory with a glint of created light? Was it the awakening power of music and words? Whatever it was, a connection was made between the longings and love in his heart and the unseen reality – the shining hosts above.

What are the intimations of divine glory in the landscape you see? In the depths of your soul? In heartfelt community expressed in song?

Bible reading
Isaiah 9:2

Prayer
Emmanuel, God with us,
Jesus, our Saviour and Lord,
may your transforming light shine in our hearts;
may we glimpse your eternal glory.

4. The Increase of Christ's Government

The Messianic words 'Of the increase of his government
. . . there shall be no end' (Isaiah 9:7, King James Version) are
read in a myriad carol services. How can this be? Tradition
has given the three magi the status of kings and has ascribed
names to them. The eighth-century monk historian Bede
described the kings this way: 'The first was called Melchior;
he was an old man, with white hair and long beard; he offered
gold to the Lord as to his king. The second, Gaspar by name,
young, beardless, of ruddy hue, offered to Jesus his gift of
incense, the homage due to Divinity. The third, of black
complexion, with heavy beard, was called Baltasar; the myrrh
he held in his hands prefigured the death of the Son of man.'
One tradition says Balthasar (an Ethiopian) was king of Arabia,
Gaspar was king of India, and Melchior was king of Persia.
Ethiopia, India and Iran once had a much stronger Christian
presence than did Europe.

> After the star, the dim day.
> After the gifts, the empty hands.
> And now we take our secret way
> Back to far lands.
>
> After the cave, the bleak plain.
> After the joy, the weary ride.
> But journey we, three new-made men
> Side by side.
>
> Came we by old paths by the sands.
> Go we by new ones this new day,
> Homewards to rule our lives and lands
> By another way.
> *A poem about the return of the three kings*
> *to their homelands, by an unknown author*

Christ's government increases on earth whenever a person moves beyond their immature self-centred ego and takes responsibility for their spheres of life – freed from the bondage of fear, rising above selfish ambition, helping to further God-led governance. These are signs that God's kingdom is breaking through.

Bible reading
Matthew 2:7-12

Prayer
Lead us in the spirit of Moses and the Wise Kings to seek just and sustaining patterns for fragile and ill-formed societies. May the royal qualities of righteousness, service and wisdom mark our governments, and may our peoples honour one another and seek the common good.

5. Eternal Life

One of the three wise men gave a gift of myrrh to the infant Jesus. Matthew, the Gospel writer, explains that this was for use at Jesus' death, a prophetic insight that somehow the greatness of this infant King was tied up with his dying as well as his living. Muslims as well as Christians believe that Jesus is the Jewish Messiah. Christians believe that his greatness and glory and eternal life come through his death – the totality of his self-giving. Heaven breaking through at a glorious death is a sign of the Uncreated Light.

An Advent theme is the Four Last Things – Death, Judgement, Heaven and Hell. St Philip Neri wrote:

'Beginners in religion ought to exercise themselves principally in meditation on the Four Last Things.'

Some friends sent this account of the death of their dear mother and wife: 'On 16 July 2015, Dana died majestically and victoriously, surrounded by love. The way in which she embraced love in her final weeks was a model of Christian witness. She was able to be present with us at our family party on 25 June serenely composed and full of love, knowing that her life on this earth was drawing to an end . . . We were able to be present at an heroic and grace-filled ending which more truly is a new beginning. Her daughter's fiancé said that it didn't feel like a death but rather Dana being set free from her body.'

On a more light-hearted note, there is the story of an old nun whom the doctor had recommended to have a tot of brandy in a cup of milk four times a day. The carer gave this to her daily, and the nun lived to be 98 years old. When she was dying, her final words were: 'For goodness sake, don't get rid of the cow.' This represents the triumph of both creation's care and humour over disintegration – indeed a sign of God's kingdom breaking through.

In the story of the man in south west Ireland (see page 69) who asked a woman how far away heaven is, she famously replied 'It's about a foot and a half above a person.' In other words, heaven is not a place, it is a dimension. It is so near it can break in at any time, but the veil is drawn aside most specially at a joyous death – truly a glimpse of glory.

Bible reading
Revelation 21:1-6

Prayer
Grant us
Death with oil,
Death with joy,
Death with light,
Death with gladness,
Death with penitence.
Shield us this and every night
Till light and dawn shall come.
                    Carmina Gadelica

6. Epiphany Hangover

Many people suffer a hangover after Christmas or New Year. Hangovers can be caused by excess food, drink or late nights. They can also be caused by memories of broken relationships, lost hopes and by loneliness. These are negative hangovers.

There is a different, entirely positive type of hangover, or rather re-hang. Art galleries hang over their walls fresh portraits and landscapes that replace over-familiar pictures. The season from Advent to Epiphany is an opportunity to look for a new re-hang that God wishes to lay before our eyes. This re-hang may be a sunrise, so fresh and unique that it takes our breath away and lifts us to a new level of awareness. It may be a physical picture by a known artist. Or it may be a visualisation that comes into focus as we pray.

Allow this re-hang to be painted in your heart. Accompany the unseen artist. Follow the lines that come from a point of darkness and those that come from a point of possibility.

Mary and Joseph nearly became part of the massacre of infants that would have included their infant Jesus. But dreams as well as treachery featured in their re-hang. They may have moved from a stable to a house in Bethlehem, yet they lost even that temporary home. However, they were welcomed into homes as refugees by the good people of Egypt. Journey, danger, unexpected hospitality featured in their re-hang. Whatever was the place they hoped to return to after their sojourn in Egypt, those hopes had to be set aside. They had to resettle in the little town of Nazareth. Jesus' father had to find a job and start a carpentry business. A hangover, or re-hang, may be about thwarted hopes, God's guidance and a new start. It may be about times of wandering and wondering – a journey with no known destination. Yet through the hammers of a workshop, through the hardship and the mundane, Heaven's patterns take form.

An epiphany reading in church lectionaries is about Jewish refugees returning to their homeland at the time of the Messiah (Jeremiah 23:6-8). Transformation of occupied territories so that exiles can return is a sign of the spreading Light. Allow a re-hang to develop before you. Let it include lostness but also leading, grief but also trust, dark but also light.

Bible reading
Matthew 2:13-23

Prayer
Divine Artist,
you uniquely shape our characters and our journeys:
endow us with gifts and pattern our lives.
May your inspired fingers work upon us,
that we may become your works of art –
your epiphany.

7. Forgiveness

The early British had a wise saying: three sources of new life – a woman's womb, a hen's egg, a wrong forgiven.

On 17 June 2015, the pastor and 13 members of Emmanuel African Methodist Episcopal Church in Charleston, USA, were in a prayer meeting. A young white racist gunned them down. Nine people died; five survived. At the court hearing, the daughter of 70-year-old murder victim Ethel Lance said to the gunman, through tears: 'You took something very precious from me. It hurts me. You hurt a lot of people, but I forgive you.' President Obama eulogised the Revd Clementa Pinckney, one of the victims, at the funeral service as a man of God who lived by faith. Obama portrayed him as a man who believed in things not seen, who believed there were better days ahead, in the distance; as a man of service who persevered knowing full well he would not receive all those things he was promised, because he believed his efforts would provide a better life for those who followed. The President, like millions of others, was so moved by the acts of forgiveness offered by these Christians that he broke into singing the hymn *Amazing Grace* which others joined in singing.

A medieval Rule of Life attributed to Saint Columba urges 'Forgiveness from the heart for everyone; constant prayers for those who trouble you.'

Mary suffered deep wounds: the massacre of innocent Bethlehem infants in a failed attempt to kill her baby; flight as refugees to Egypt; the betrayal, torture and untimely death of her most noble son. Yet she, like her son who cried out before he expired 'Father, forgive them, for they know not what they do', forgave from the heart. As a result, she had space in her heart to love everyone with deepest insight. She became a spiritual mother to the world.

Forgiveness still releases and illuminates spiritual powers that would otherwise remain in limbo. Forgiveness is not about forgetting what happened or letting the ill-doer off the hook. It is seeing the perpetrator through new eyes. It is a gift to ourselves as well as to the other.

There is a saying that refusing to forgive someone is like drinking poison every day in the hope that eventually the other person will die. This damages our chances of sustaining joy and healthy, happy relationships.

Forgiveness releases a form of epiphany.

Bible reading
Luke 1:60-77

Prayer
Grant us the grace of forgiveness that we may harvest relationships of trust,

gentleness and generosity – and restore the light in our eyes.

8. New Year: Unlocking Greatness

At the New Year I sent this as my daily prayer tweet: 'Lighten our heavy steps as we trudge through this grey and terror-prone year, for the glory of God is now among us.'[19]

'The King is among us', we sing. Who is this king? 'Great David's greater Son'.

What is a sign of his presence? He unlocks the greatness in his subjects. How?

One way is to inspire us to make a New Year resolution or to try something fresh. At New Year a former Scottish rugby player with brawn but joints stiff with the scars of injuries joined a yoga class. He learned to become supple. A blind person bloated with a beer belly took up swimming. Others realise that a body beautiful is an insufficient goal. War veterans with amputated limbs decide to become coaches of under-motivated young people rather than to become depressed couch potatoes.

To set goals and engage in an adventure of possibility is better than to turn inwards or slide downwards. However, if we do these in our own strength, people see in us only the ephemeral glory of the old Adam, not the real glory of the New Adam.

In 1908 Minnie Louise Haskins wrote a poem whose popular title is *The Gate of the Year*. It caught the public imagination when the then Princess Elizabeth handed a copy to her father, King George VI, and he quoted it in his 1939 Christmas broadcast. Its words have remained a source of comfort for Queen Elizabeth, who celebrated her 90th birthday in 2016. The secret revealed in this poem is that we may walk hand in hand with a Higher Power.

---

19. See https://twitter.com/praycelticdaily

The seeker asks the man who stands at the gate of the year to give him a light that he may tread safely into the unknown. He tells him to go into the darkness and put his hand into the Hand of God, for that will be better than darkness and safer than a known way.

The poem finishes with the Hand of God leading the man to the breaking of day in the East.

Bible reading
Psalm 24

Prayer
At the gate of the year we put our hands in yours.
As the old tide recedes, may we learn from you how our journey should be
and follow your footsteps planted in fresh sands.

9. The Theophany of Baptism

When I dialogue with friendly Muslim evangelists on the streets they usually start by saying that God cannot be divided. They get me to agree that Christ admitted he was ignorant about many things. They conclude that God cannot be ignorant; therefore Christ cannot be God. I sometimes say to them: 'God is not a Problem to be solved but a Mystery to be entered into – let's be open to the Mystery.' Or I talk about the Muslims' 99 names or attributes of God. I might say, 'I believe God is both the Hidden One and the Manifest One – do you?'

The Feast of the Holy Theophany (Epiphany) of our Lord God and Saviour Jesus Christ is celebrated each year on 6 January. On that day, Orthodox churches commemorate the Baptism of Christ and the divine revelation of the Holy Trinity; other branches of the Church celebrate that later. At the Baptism of Christ, all three Persons of the Holy Trinity – Father, Son, and Holy Spirit – were made manifest.

When Jesus came up from the water, the heavens opened suddenly, and the Holy Spirit descended upon him. The Bible records that the Spirit descended like a dove and alighted on him. When this happened, a voice came from heaven and said, 'This is my Son, the Beloved, with whom I am well pleased' (Matthew 3:17). This was the voice of God the Father.

Christ's baptism in the Jordan was 'theophany', a manifestation of God to the world, because it was the beginning of our Lord's public ministry. It was also a 'theophany' in that the world was granted a revelation of the Holy Trinity. All three Persons were made manifest together: the Father testified from on high to the divine (non-biological) Sonship of Jesus; the Son received his Father's testimony; and the Spirit was seen in the form of a dove, descending from the Father and resting upon the Son.

At Epiphany people dive into rivers or seas to retrieve a cross that has been buried beneath the waters, to symbolise Christ rising in glory. The words 'Christ has appeared and enlightened the world' are often sung. Therefore, 6 January is also known as the Feast of Lights. The Church celebrates on this day the illumination of the world by the light of Christ. Countless people of other faiths or none have come into an experience of theophany. They have heard a voice, felt a presence or seen the light.

Bible reading
Mark 1:9-11

Prayer
As Christ enters the stream of created life,
we are immersed in the stream of divine life.
As Christ comes up out of the water,
the world is charged with the glory of God.
Saviour, immerse in your Presence our lives, our lands,
our world.

10. The Wonder of Light

These 40 days of readings began with the trepidations of Advent darkness. They end with the transforming wonder of Light. Properties of created light include radiation, energy, radio waves, heat, and x-rays. The light that we see every day is only a fraction of the light emitted by the sun. Visible light is emitted through tiny packets called photons. Light can play a significant part in wound therapy. It creates vitamin D and speeds the production of various healing agents. The properties of Uncreated Light are even greater in their effects. This spiritual light often evokes a sense of revelation and wonder, and it can be triggered by something in our experience – for example, a birth. A church member, a scientist, had once been an atheist. I asked her what had brought her to faith. 'The birth of my first child,' she said, 'it was such a wonderful experience.'

The astronaut Ed Mitchell experienced a moment of transformative wonder as he travelled back to earth from the moon: 'There was an overwhelming sense of oneness, of connectedness; it wasn't "Them and Us", it was "That's me!", that's all of it . . . it's one thing. And it was accompanied by an ecstasy, a sense of "Oh my God, wow, yes", an insight, an epiphany.[20] Mitchell's life was forever changed by this epiphany experience.

Jesus said: 'I am the light of the world' (John 8:12). Saint Patrick described Jesus as the True Sun. The universal (Nicene) church creed describes the Lord Jesus Christ, Son of God, as Light of Light. Something of this light, however dimmed, is in every human being (John 1:4). Countless converts, like Paul of Tarsus who experienced sudden conversion on the

---

20. From the 2000 documentary *In the Shadow of the Moon*, Discovery Films, Film 4.

Damascus road, say they 'saw the light'. To 'see the light' in English means to understand something that you previously did not.

Darkness cannot drive out darkness; only light can do that, as Dr Martin Luther King and many others have pointed out. J.K. Rowling made the point in *Harry Potter and the Order of the Phoenix* that everyone has both dark and light inside them. What matters is the part we choose to act on. That makes us who we are.

> O Star of wonder, star of night,
> Star with royal beauty bright,
> Westward leading, still proceeding,
> Guide us to thy Perfect Light.

Bible reading
Isaiah 60:1-3, 19-22

Prayer
As day follows night, may we be bathed in your Light.
Fill the world with people who shine
even in darkest corner and deepest pit
until the world is filled with your glory, as the waters cover the sea.